COVENANT • BIBLE • STUDIES

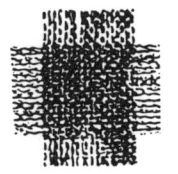

Wisdom

Christopher Bowman

faithQuest™ ✦ Brethren Press™

Copyright © 1995 by *faithQuest*. Published by Brethren Press, 1451 Dundee Avenue, Elgin, IL 60120

Brethren Press and *faithQuest* are trademarks of the Church of the Brethren General Board.

All rights reserved. No portion of this book may be reproduced in any form or by any process or technique without the written consent of the publisher, except for brief quotations embodied in critical articles or reviews.

Unless otherwise noted, scripture quotations are from the New Revised Standard Version of the Bible, copyrighted 1989 by the National Council of Churches of Christ in the USA, Division of Education and Ministry.

Cover photo by Don Ford

99 98 97 96 95   5 4 3 2 1

Library of Congress Cataloging-in-Publication Data

Bowman, Christopher D., 1962-
   Wisdom / Christopher D. Bowman.
      p. cm. — (Covenant Bible study series)
   Includes bibliographical references.
   ISBN 0-87178-944-2 (pbk.)
   1. Wisdom literature. 2. Wisdom—Biblical teaching. 3. Wisdom—Religious aspects—Christianity. I. Title. II. Series.
BS1455.B65 1995
229'.306—dc20   95-18011

Manufactured in the United States of America

Contents

Foreword vii
Preface ix
1. What Is Wisdom? 1
2. Practical Wisdom 7
3. Wisdom Has Its Rewards 13
4. When the Innocent Suffer 17
5. Responding to Pain 23
6. Searching for Meaning in Our World 27
7. Finding Meaning in a World That
   Is Not Always Fair 33
8. Wise Advice for the Well-to-Do 39
9. Friendship 45
10. Wise Advice in an Age of Anxiety 51
Suggestions for Sharing and Prayer 57

Foreword

The Covenant Bible Study Series was first developed for a denominational program in the Church of the Brethren and the Christian Church (Disciples of Christ). This program, called People of the Covenant, was founded on the concept of relational Bible study and has been adopted by several other denominations and small groups who want to study the Bible in a community rather than alone.

Relational Bible study is marked by certain characteristics, some of which differ from other types of Bible study. For one, it is intended for small groups of people who can meet face-to-face on a regular basis and share frankly with an intimate group.

It is important to remember that relational Bible study is anchored in covenantal history. God covenanted with people in Old Testament history, established a new covenant in Jesus Christ, and covenants with the church today.

Relational Bible study takes seriously a corporate faith. As each person contributes to study, prayer, and work, the group becomes the real body of Christ. Each one's contribution is needed and important. "For just as the body is one and has many members, and all the members of the body, though many, are one body, so it is with Christ. . . . Now you are the body of Christ and individually members of it" (1 Cor. 12:12, 17).

Relational Bible study helps both individuals and the group to claim the promise of the Spirit and the working of the Spirit. As one person testified, "In our commitment to one another and in our sharing, something happened. . . . We were woven together in love by the master Weaver. It is something that can happen only when two or three or seven are gathered in God's name, and we know the promise of God's presence in our lives."

The symbol for these covenant Bible study groups is the burlap cross. The interwoven threads, the uniqueness of each strand, the unrefined fabric, and the rough texture characterize covenant groups. The people in the groups are unique but interrelated; they are imperfect and unpolished, but loving and supportive.

The shape that these divergent threads create is the cross, the symbol for all Christians of the resurrection and presence with us of Christ our Savior. Like the burlap cross, we are brought together, simple and ordinary, to be sent out again in all directions to be in the world.

For people who choose to use this study in a small group, the following guidelines will help create an atmosphere in which support will grow and faith will deepen.

1. As a small group of learners, we gather around God's word to discern its meaning for today.
2. The words, stories, and admonitions we find in scripture come alive for today, challenging and renewing us.
3. All people are learners and all are leaders.
4. Each person will contribute to the study, sharing the meaning found in the scripture and helping to bring meaning to others.
5. We recognize each other's vulnerability as we share out of our own experience, and in sharing we learn to trust others and to be trustworthy.

Additional suggestions for study and group-building are provided in the "Sharing and Prayer" section. They are intended for use in the hour preceding the Bible study to foster intimacy in the covenant group and relate personal sharing to the Bible study topic.

Welcome to this study. As you search the scriptures, may you also search yourself. May God's voice and guidance and the love and encouragement of brothers and sisters in Christ challenge you to live more fully the abundant life God promises.

Preface

Wisdom literature holds a unique place in the biblical tradition. While other styles of scripture emphasize spectacular, supernatural stories about God's activity, wisdom uses the common-sense approach to call us to full life. It is not that God is not important, but, as human beings, the choices we make, the work we do, and the lives we lead make a difference and direct our future.

Sounding a great deal like works righteousness, these scripture selections preach that what we do matters. Doing the right things leads to life. Doing the wrong things leads to death. Wisdom is simply the instruction manual for life.

In this book we will look at what it means to choose wisely. Do good choices bring good results, or is all our striving vain? We will also look at the challenge of innocent suffering: If we believe that good behavior brings goodness, why do good people suffer? And through it all, we will ask each other for insights and observations about our own life choices.

—Christopher Bowman

Recommended Resources

Brueggeman, Walter. *In Man We Trust: The Neglected Side of Biblical Faith.* Westminster John Knox, 1972.

Crenshaw, James L. *Old Testament Wisdom: An Introduction.* Westminster John Knox, 1981.

Farmer, Kathleen A. *Proverbs and Ecclesiastes: Who Knows What Is Good?* Eerdmans, 1991.

Von Rad, Gerhard. *Wisdom in Israel.* Abingdon Press, 1972.

1

What Is Wisdom?
Proverbs 1:1-33

Revelation is knowing God through mighty acts that defy the natural order of things. Wisdom is knowing God is present simply in the order, patterns, and common sense of the created world. We often forget, or don't realize, that wisdom is a phenomenal way to know God.

Personal Preparation

1. Browse through the Book of Proverbs. Take note of any references to God. What, if anything, is God doing in this book?
2. Read Proverbs 1:1-33. How did you respond when adults tried to impart wisdom to you as a teenager? How do youth respond to you today when you try to warn them of life's pitfalls?
3. Reflect on a recent choice you have made concerning your life's direction. How did you arrive at your decision? How was God active in your choosing?

Understanding

I ask no dream, no prophet ecstasies,
no sudden rending of the veil of clay,
no angel visitant, no op'ning skies,
but take the dimness of my soul away.
—from "Spirit of God! Descend" by George Croly

During the last year of college, I struggled with the question of calling. My heart felt inclined toward set-apart ministry in the church. Yet, having read biblical reports of calling, I expected something more than an inclination.

I expected earthquakes, angels, opening skies, or prophetic utterances. I wanted to see angels like Isaiah saw and hear God's voice like Jeremiah heard (Isa. 6; Jer. 1:5-9). I begged for flaming chariots (2 Kings 2), lightening bolts (Acts 9), or at least some of Gideon's damp fleece (Judg. 6). I really expected my call to be something other than divine silence.

Then a wise friend said, "I don't know why you are confused. You obviously enjoy religion classes. You have a natural interest in the Bible. And of the friends I have at college, you alone have been *pastor* to me. I think your calling is obvious."

It began to dawn on me that God-driven choices may not require divine intervention. Although God may at times grant lightening-bolt revelations and miraculous visions, correct choice does not always require a visit from God. Sometimes the natural patterns of our common-sense experience in God's good creation give us enough confidence to know what is right.

The idea that people can make good choices without God's intervention runs counter to what we are often led to believe. When facing difficult choices, we are more apt to ask God to step in and choose for us. Is it biblical to suggest that we can make correct decisions without God's direct intervention?

A Nigerian proverb claims, "The Bible is like the elephant. Open it and you find everything inside." Every part of the elephant from tusk to tail is useful. And every part of the Bible is useful in giving us a full picture of God. The prophets preach God's judgment against evil. The priests lead us to know God through worship. Abraham and Moses show us something of who God is through covenants, laws, and commandments. And the stories of the people of Israel demonstrate that our God is active in the human story. Each point of view reveals a different part of God to us and shows us that God is active in the created order.

Wisdom sayings and stories are yet another way of knowing God. They teach that God's path of righteousness is discovered through observation, not revelation. Rather than speaking directly to the people about things, God saturated creation with truth and gave us ways to understand it. We learn what is good not from a verbose deity, but by keeping our eyes open and our mouths shut (Prov. 15:28).

Books listed as wisdom literature are Proverbs, Job, Ecclesiastes, and some of Psalms. In the Apocrypha (holy scriptures that are not included in all versions of the Bible), Sirach (Ecclesiasticus) and the Wisdom of Solomon are also wisdom books. Some scholars would add Song of Songs, Ruth, Tobit, parts of Deuteronomy, Esther, and Amos. Even the story of Joseph (Gen. 37—50, but omitting 38 and 49) is considered a wisdom story which, without visible intervention by God, teaches about virtue.

New Testament sayings and moral teachings of Jesus, such as those found in the Sermon on the Mount, are a type of wisdom literature, as is John's Gospel and the Letter of James. Here, too, people are called on to make right decisions based upon what they observe rather than upon divine revelation. While only some people experience divine revelations, and then only at God's choosing, wisdom is available to all who will come to their senses and learn to choose the right path.

I didn't understand the importance of wisdom when I was searching for my calling. And as a church, we don't often understand the importance of the wisdom tradition, which affirms the world, celebrates culture, looks to our surroundings for truth, and calls for human responsibility. Within these writings are sayings similar to those my grandmother used when I was foolish. There is an undeniable logic in expressions such as "haste makes waste" and "in for a penny; in for a pound." Here is truth available to anyone who will listen.

In the novel *Cold Sassy Tree* by Olive Burns, Will almost gets run over by a train. He asks, "Grandpa, you think I'm alive tonight 'cause it was God's will?"

"Naw, you livin' cause you had the good sense to fall down 'twixt them tracks."

"Maybe God give me the idea."

"You can believe thet, son, if'n you think it was God's idea for you to be up on thet there trestle in the first place. What God gave you was a brain. Hit's His will for you to use it p'tickler when a train's comin' " (p. 97).

There comes a time when adult children stop hugging teddy bears and blaming parents for the ills that plague them. Theologically, as well, there comes a time when we claim responsibility for our actions. We no longer sit, surrounded by the life rafts of creation and experience, idly waiting for God to rescue us. We begin to see what tools (observation and reason) God has given us to use in life. Wisdom does not remove God from power, but rather refuses to remove humans from responsibility.

The goal of wisdom is that the young learn prudence, the simple learn shrewdness, and the wise acquire skill (1:4-5). The Hebrew word for "acquire skill" has meanings ranging from twisting the ropes of sails in order to steer the boat, to the writhing of a woman in childbirth. In both cases hard work, coupled with maturity and patience, brings a new way and new life.

Wisdom does not present a new set of laws or rules that God sets down. In fact, some of the sayings contradict each other, such as Proverbs 26:4-5, which says do answer fools and don't answer fools. Instead, wisdom wants to set us on the right path by using reason and good judgment. In this way wisdom is no different from the priests and the prophets. They all want us to join the kingdom of righteousness, justice, and equity (Prov. 1:3). They simply have their own ways of walking down that path.

Wisdom is personified in Hebrew as a woman who cries to the people, "How long, O simple ones, will you love being simple?" (1:22). That reminds us of the prophet calling "How long shall your evil schemes lodge within you?" (Jer. 4:14). As she delivers her message at the city gates (Prov.1:21), we remember other life-changing events that took place there (Ruth 4:11; Ps. 69:12). And as she calls us to turn from our simple ways (1:22), we remember another call to repent and make a straight path (Isa. 40:3; Matt. 3:3).

As we address the realities of life and search for the right way to go, we find invitations to the kingdom of God in the observations of the wise ones of old. Those who struggled with death, pain, suffering, and travail during the time of exile in Babylon or in Israel thousands of years ago asked the same questions and felt the same pain as those suffering in Babylon and Israel today. These are the questions we share regardless of technological advancements or the passing of time. These are the questions of life. The invitation of Wisdom is to leave our disoriented lives and receive her teachings. It is yet another invitation into the kingdom of God.

Discussion and Action

1. Remember some of the proverbs and sayings you learned as a child. Talk about their usefulness in your life and in your faith.
2. Reread chapter 1 of Proverbs. Name some obvious ways this book of the Bible differs from other books.
3. What references to God do you find in Proverbs 1? How is God acting in the lives of the people who read Proverbs?
4. If you can, share with the group a decision you now face. What tools or insights do you think God has provided to help you make that decision? What tools or insights do you possess that are visible to the group?
5. Who do you think possesses the most wisdom? Is it the old, the young, the poor, the wealthy, or the educated? What are the signs of a wise person?
6. Reflect on the difference between revelation and observation. How has God come to you most often? In miraculous ways? In ordinary ways? Share with the group about a time in your past when God helped to direct your path through observation rather than revelation—through practical insight rather than lightening bolts and earthquakes.

7. Thinking back over the last few sermons you've heard, would you say they sound more like Psalms, Deuteronomy, Paul's letters, or Proverbs? Why? How does your congregation work to bring the good news to people in practical ways?
8. Begin, as a group, to collect and list favorite wisdom sayings from the Bible and from our culture. Plan to talk to elderly folks, other adults, youth, and children about wise sayings they know. Appoint a recorder to update this list each week and highlight group favorites.

2

Practical Wisdom
Proverbs 10:1—22:16

How do we know what the truth is? What seems wise in one setting is not necessarily wise in another. Instead of answers, God has given us wisdom to search for the truth.

Personal Preparation

1. Browse through Proverbs 10:1—22:16. Underline some of the proverbs with which you agree. Place an X beside some of those sayings with which you disagree. Place a question mark beside the ones that are problematic for you.
2. Which proverbs have you used? Which ones have been used against you?
3. Think of a disagreement you've had with someone in which both of you were right to some extent. How does that affect the way you think of truth?

Understanding

Wisdom literature, especially in the Book of Proverbs, is the common-sense approach to religion. This is no flowery worded, highfalutin doctrine of which angels sing. This is theology that we can roll up our sleeves and get to work with. This is blue-collar, dirt-under-the-fingernails, meat-and-potatoes stuff. Here is the practical advice for life—good stuff for the people in the pew who have historically distrusted theologians. No need to work at understanding the mysteries of sanctification, eschatology, or defining the mysteries of the incarnation—this is stuff you simply understand and live. It is the shoe commercial of theology: "Just Do It!" Actions speak louder than words (20:11).

This particular collection of proverbs brings together the oldest sayings in the book. There is no special order to the sayings, and some are more easily understood by people of our time than are others. Each couplet is meant to be read and understood as a reiteration of the underlying theme: life offers us choices between good and bad. The proverbs help us to see that right moral choices lead to life in fullness while following evil leads to ruin.

Wisdom literature does not doubt that God is good. Nor does it imply that God is absent. It simply argues that, for human beings, the choices we make, the work we do, and the lives we lead make a difference, good or bad, in the fulfillment of our lives. That is not to say we can control everything about our lives. It only acknowledges that our decisions affect in some way whether our life will be full or empty.

There is an old story about a retired man who bought a piece of land just outside of town. The new owner spent hours working on the grounds, clearing the land and bringing some order to the chaos of overgrown vegetation. After months of toil, the land flourished. A friend stopped by and remarked, "It's a wonderful piece of land you and God have here." To which the tired grounds keeper replied, "I suppose. But you should have seen it when God was going it alone."

While wisdom emphasizes the importance of a person's actions, it does not diminish the role of God in human events. After all, it was God who created humans and gave us many powers and abilities. When these are at work, they are evidence of God's handiwork, not ours. And when we are virtuous, we are instruments of God's virtue at work in the world. "Crooked minds are an abomination to the Lord, but those of blameless ways are his delight" (11:20). Recognizing that in the end everything comes from God, Proverbs 19:23 tells us that the good life is based not on being wise by ourselves, but on honoring God:

Practical Wisdom

"The fear of the Lord is life indeed; filled with it one rests secure and suffers no harm" (see also 14:26-27; 15:33; 21:30). But what is this virtue that shows God's hand in the world? Is voluntary poverty a virtue? Are wealth and prosperity signs of virtue? Is service the highest virtue a Christian can hold? Interestingly, wisdom does not rush to defend the rich, but neither is there condemnation of wealth.

Material wealth (riches) is seen as a blessing from God (10:22) as well as the result of hard work (10:4). In general, riches are better than poverty (18:11, 23; 19:4, 6-7), but poverty is better than greed, injustice, or foolishness (10:2; 11:7, 24-26; 15:16; 16:16, 19; 17:16; 19:1, 22; 20:15; 21:6). Wealth is manifest in a variety of ways (material possessions, good morals, good relationships), and wisdom places these in the proper perspective.

Care for the poor is seen as an obligation and a divine mandate. "Whoever is kind to the poor lends to the Lord, and will be repaid in full" (19:17; see also 14:21; 17:5 and 21:13). Help and repayment in the wisdom tradition is a natural occurrence between people who care for each other, knowing that others will willingly care for them when the time comes. Working together in such a way is a natural progression of life. Perhaps the reward is in the inherent blessing of doing acts of kindness. Perhaps it is the winning of friends. Perhaps it is the peace in one's soul. But television preachers, for example, who use this passage (19:17) to ask for money for their "struggling" ministries and add the promise that God will "double your money," are certainly speaking outside the biblical meaning.

Even though wisdom is often common sensical and a natural progression of life, it is also tricky in some cases. Just as our own cultural sayings are contradictory, so is biblical wisdom. In 10:4 we read that hard work brings riches, but later in that same chapter (10:22) we read that the blessing of God brings wealth. An even more blatant example of contradiction is found in 26:4-5: "Do not answer fools according to their folly, or you will be a fool yourself. Answer fools according to their folly, or they will be wise in their own eyes." How can this be? Is not truth always true? Well, yes and no.

We nod in knowing appreciation when, after Thanksgiving dinner, Grandma pronounces, "Many hands make light work," but we also understand the wisdom in her words an hour earlier when, chasing us from the aromatic kitchen, she proclaimed, "Too many cooks spoil the broth."

Under the influence of turkey-overdose, we begin to wonder if we should insist that Grandma be consistent. If too many hands were a curse prior to dinner, why are they helpful now? Shouldn't Grandma be held accountable for such inconsistency? Are these not in direct contradiction? And yet, are they not both "true"?

The sages of old were not leaving the judgment of right and wrong to the individual person in the individual moment; neither did they insist that every problem had a clearly right or wrong answer according to divine legal prescriptions. Instead, the truth that is presented by wisdom is a truth with all the ambiguity of reality. Truth is not located completely in each person's judgment (16:2). Nor is truth completely outside of us (21:30). Instead, truth is found by the people searching together and attending together to the reality which they find. Together we are given the ear that hears and the eye that sees both given by the Lord (20:12).

Discussion and Action

1. Share some of the sayings you marked in the preparation exercise. Try to clarify the ones people marked with a question mark. Name a few ways you would like to use the sayings with which you agree.
2. Find a few biblical proverbs that contradict one another. Also mention modern proverbs that are contradictory. Add them to your list of collected sayings. Explain the way in which each might be true. Are there situations where both might be true even though in contradiction?
3. Try your hand at defining truth. Someone once said never let your sense of morals prevent you from doing what is right. Describe situations where things usually

thought of as wrong might be right. How do we know which is which?
4. Consider whether it is always wrong to lie, even if you could save a life by doing it. Consider whether it is always wrong to work on the sabbath, even if your family would go hungry because of it. Consider whether divorce is always wrong, even in cases where one spouse is adulterous. How does our perception of the truth change in situations like these?
5. When have you seen wealth (material wealth, moral wealth, or relational wealth) as a blessing from God? When have you seen someone prosper because they were a dedicated worker? Is our abundance a blessing from God or luck?
6. Recall some wise sayings from your grandparents and add them to your list. Also, try your hand at writing your own proverbs to share with the group.

Send someone from your group to talk to your church newsletter editor. Suggest that the newsletter carry a proverb on each page. Bring along a list of suggestions gleaned from your group's list of favorites. Consider including a year-end "Top Ten" list of proverbs.

3

Wisdom Has Its Rewards
Proverbs 3

Proverbs 3 claims that wisdom has rewards and foolishness has its price. Still, we all know that even wise people suffer. But despite inevitable troubles in our lives, we also know that in the end the wise way is always preferable.

Personal Preparation

1. In what ways does the hymn below accurately reflect a central truth of faith? How might this hymn be too simplistic in its understanding of faith?

   When we walk with the Lord
       in the light of his word,
         what a glory he sheds on our way!
   While we do his good will,
       he abides with us still,
         and with all who will trust and obey.

   —from "When We Walk with the Lord" by John H. Sammis

2. Read Proverbs 3. Think of a time in your life when you questioned whether wisdom made any difference. What made you choose good judgment in the end?

3. Find the sections of Proverbs as outlined below. These sections came from different times and different generations. Think about the difference in the wisdom of your generation and the generation ahead or behind you.

Understanding

The Book of Proverbs is made up of different collections of sayings from a variety of sources and times. We can outline the book in the following way:

1:1—9:18	Wisdom poems and instructions
10:1—22:16	"The Proverbs of Solomon"
22:17—24:34	"The Words of the Wise" (from Egyptian texts)
25:1—29:27	"More 'Proverbs of Solomon,' Copied by the Men of Hezekiah, King of Judah"
30:1-14	"The Words of Agur, Son of Jakeh"
30:15-33	untitled numerical sayings
31:1-9	"Words of Lemuel, King of Massa, Which His Mother Taught Him"
31:10-31	an acrostic poem on the woman of worth

With this configuration it is clear that the Book of Proverbs need not be read straight through. A variety of styles and sayings are gathered here; some are even from outside the Hebrew tradition. Each verse is to be savored and understood before moving to the next. As the proverb says, "If you have found honey, eat only enough for you, or else, having too much, you will vomit it" (25:16).

Regardless of style and source, however, each of the proverbs in these sections carries a common theme: Following these instructions leads to real rewards. The rewards, according to Proverbs 3, come in the form of health (vv. 2, 8, 16), wealth (vv. 10, 16), safety (vv. 23, 25-26), faith (vv. 4, 6, 32-35), contentment (vv. 17-18), and honor (vv. 4, 16, 35). The path of wisdom brings reward not through divine intervention, but because that's the way things have been woven together in the very fabric of creation (vv. 19-20; see 8:22-36).

It is important to remember, in our reflection on these proverbs, that the ancient Israelites did not concern themselves with an elaborate belief in an afterlife. They did not have a "postponement" theology in which rewards and punishments were held over for the next world. Likewise, the rewards and punishments that are the consequences of our behavior are realized in this life, not in some heaven or hell. The action takes place in this life and so do the results. Both are evident in the here and now.

God is not a vending machine but, to a certain extent, the world is—put in the right money, pull the right lever, and out comes the candy. Good choices lead to prosperity and bad decisions lead to destruction. As the scripture says, this outcome seems to be caused by God sometimes (3:26). At other times, Wisdom herself is the source of the prosperity (3:16). Either way, the world reacts in predictable ways to the actions people take. In fact, Proverbs 3:33 promises that "the Lord's curse is on the house of the wicked, but he blesses the abode of the righteous."

Not long ago our children received a toy fire engine which is made to be taken apart and reassembled by three-year-olds. Being good parents, my wife and I decided to assemble the toy ourselves and judge whether or not it was appropriate for our children. When we finally got the fire engine together, there was one screw left on the floor. Chuckling with each other, we disassembled and reassembled the toy, paying special attention to what we might have missed. We decided that if it was made for a three-year-old, parents should certainly be able to figure it out.

After seven or eight attempts, we had no success. After each assembly, the lonely screw was still on the floor, seeming to laugh at us. At the peak of our frustration, we finally decided to read the instructions—only to find that the kit included one extra screw.

Going through life can be like that. We are often convinced that we've got a screw loose when all we need to do is read the instructions. Our own life experiences show us that trust and obedience have their rewards. Following instructions and obeying rules, even when difficult, are essential to living fully.

The mother, in the midst of labor's pain, must be instructed to wait, breathe, then push. The person recovering from open heart surgery must learn a new way of living, exercising, and eating. Couples seeking counseling rely on the insights and experience of a counselor who will suggest changes in behavior and give instructions for living. Without instruction, we might well harm ourselves or others. Especially on the frontiers of our experience, where we possess just a little knowledge, we need to pay special attention to the instructions of those who have gone before us and, like teenagers, learn to know the rules of the road before we jump into the car (3:1, 11, 21).

While obedience to rules and the teachings of our ancestors is only a small part of faith, it is an important part. If we were to do only a portion of what we are advised in the wisdom writings of the Bible, we would be better off, but we do not even do that much at times. In our eagerness for dramatic faith and profound religious experience, we have overlooked the simple and fulfilling rewards of Christian obedience.

Discussion and Action

1. Tell about times in your life when obedience was rewarding even if it was difficult.
2. Rules for life, such as the ones in Proverbs 3, may relieve us from having to make wise decisions on our own. On the other hand, rules can also be a burden. When do you find it liberating to follow wise rules? When is it confining?
3. For the most part wise decisions will lead to reward, although some pain in life is unavoidable. Discuss whether it is always preferable to be wise, even though pain and suffering are inevitable.
4. Look together at the different sections of Proverbs. Note the differences in style in each section. Then talk about the differences in the wisdom of different generations today. What wisdom do adults have to offer? What wisdom do youth have? How are little children wise?
5. Acknowledge one place in your life where you know you should do (or stop doing) something. Write your acknowledgment on an index card and share it with one other person if you are able. As a pair, promise to keep tabs on these areas for each other as each person resolves to act (or stop acting) on their issue.

4

When the Innocent Suffer
Job 1—2; 3—7

When bad things happen to bad people, we think justice is finally being done. When good things happen to good people, we feel that rewards are finally being given. But what is going on when good things happen to bad people or bad things happen to good people?

Personal Preparation
1. Look over chapters 1—7 of Job. When have you been tempted to blame God for your trouble? How has God been a help to you in your suffering?
2. How has pain and suffering—your own or someone else's—affected your faith?
3. Pray daily for people who are suffering pain or unjust treatment.

Understanding
In 1986 I took my clinical pastoral education experience in a large hospital on the edge of Chicago. Our chaplaincy group—a Methodist supervisor, three Brethren, a Baptist, two nuns, and a priest—tried always to take a religious look at things in a world of medical priorities.

In general we fared well. We think we helped patients and families probe the deepest questions in life as they faced great pain and sometimes death. We witnessed births, deaths, violence, disease, and healing and were there to help people express joy, sorrow, anger, despair, and faith.

On at least one occasion, however, we had no uplifting, quick answer. An infant was brought to the emergency room with a piece of apple lodged in her windpipe. She couldn't breathe. The hospital staff might have been able to save her had they known she had earlier lost one lung in another accident. In a moment she was gone. For many of us, her death tore at the very fabric of faith.

Out of our natural and deep sense of justice, we know that babies don't deserve to die. Murderers, smokers, gang members, and people not wearing seatbelts may be culpable, but not innocent babies. This is the confession that tugs at our heartstrings when we witness child abuse, when we see starving infants, and when we hear of children held hostage by terrorists or divorcing parents. These children have done nothing to deserve their fate.

Much of our thinking is governed by a simplistic theology of judgment. If something is going wrong, we look back to find where it was that we stepped out of bounds. Just as Joshua had to retrace his steps following defeat at Ai (Josh. 7), as David was forced to deal with the sin of the nation (2 Sam. 21), and the sailors transporting Jonah searched for the storm-causing sin (Jon. 1), we easily attribute rotten luck to bad living. Yet, often this is not enough.

The Book of Job wrestles with this question. This is the story of a blameless man who praises God for his many blessings. God knows that Job can sing praises easily because he is healthy, prosperous, and happy. But God wonders if Job could still praise his Lord if he were afflicted with pain. When Job becomes covered with sores and suffers terribly, he struggles with the reason for his travail. Much of the book is taken up with the speeches of well-meaning friends who try to uncover the sin that is making Job suffer. Job insists on his innocence (a claim confirmed by the narrator).

No matter how divine the revelation, traditional the dogma, or liberal the faith, each person usually experiences a moment when God's actions do not seem to make sense. In these very moments we become wrestlers, battling with the Divine. Like Job, and Jacob before him (Gen. 32:23-33), we wrestle throughout the night. Struggling with all our might, we ask only for a blessing in the dawn. Sometimes, through God's goodness, we are given not only a blessing, but a new name and a new way of living.

At other times, the suffering continues. The more difficult it is to endure, the more we feel the very foundation of our faith shaken. In the face of terrible loss or illness, we ask ourselves, What did I do to deserve this? Sometimes we need to assume responsibility for what happens in our lives, but often we must remember the story of Job in which we are told once and for all that suffering is not always punishment for sin; people do not always deserve the pain they receive.

In fact, Job's suffering was due to his virtue; he was too good for his own good (1:8). He was faithful because he was blessed. Now he was being tested to see if he could be faithful even when things were not so good. This lesson is repeated when the disciples ask Jesus whether the man's blindness in John 9 was punishment for someone's sin. Jesus' answer is that the blameless blind man was afflicted in order to prepare him to reveal God. Sometimes God does not provide the answer—God is the answer.

A woman and her husband, pillars of the church, active volunteers in the community, and compassionate Christian people, were awaiting the test results following surgery on the husband for skin cancer (malignant melanoma). Of their three children, both sons had died of cancer. Their daughter had recently undergone a mastectomy after being diagnosed with breast cancer. Friends of the family commented, "You are such good people; why is this happening to you?" The woman's reply was, "Well! Why not us?" Here she struck upon a central observation of faith. Why Job in his ashes? Why Paul in his suffering? Why Naomi in her loss? Why Jesus on the cross?

Whether we like it or not, pain is a part of the human condition within creation. The good news for us is that God's activity has less to do with the production of, or protection from, pain and more to do with making pain something less than the final word in our story. The joy in the resurrection story is not that death did not happen, or that it will never happen again, but that death no longer has the final word.

The friends of Job clung so strongly to their concepts of God that they refused to respond appropriately to Job's anger and pain. The idolatry of tradition limited their ability to see God's mystery in a new way. Likewise, many of us, when visiting a friend in pain, are more interested in protecting our preconceived notions of God than we are in protecting the sacred space of pain in which God's mystery is often revealed.

While the initial lesson learned from the Book of Job is that sometimes innocent people suffer, an equally important lesson is that ministry to those in pain should not place the idolatry of theology or tradition before the patience of trust in God. At one point or another, we are called simply to be in relationship with suffering and trust in God's goodness.

Jewish theologian Abraham Heschel writes in his book, *A Passion for Truth:*

> God needs not only sympathy and comfort, but partners, silent warriors. . . . God does not need those who praise him when in a state of euphoria. He needs those who are in love with him when in distress. . . . This is the task: in the darkest night to be certain of the dawn, certain of the power to turn a curse into a blessing, agony into a song. To know the monster's rage and, in spite of it, proclaim to its face (even a monster will be transfigured into an angel); to go through hell and to continue to trust in the goodness of God—this is the challenge and the way.

Discussion and Action

1. Who is Satan? Is he the anti-Christ? a servant of God? How do you react, knowing God allowed Satan to bring suffering on Job? What does it mean to you that the Satan is part of the gathering and discussions of the Son of God?

2. Tell about times when friends have offered you answers. Were they helpful? unhelpful? When have you tried to offer answers to a friend? Were you helpful? unhelpful?
3. Talk about Abraham Heschel's words. Together name the "monsters" of life and the "monsters' rage" which you encounter in life.
4. "Pain, the gift nobody wants"—have you ever thought of pain as a gift? Name some times when this has been true for you.
5. List ways that Christians proclaim the certainty of the dawn.
6. If death is not the final word, what is the final word for people of faith?
7. Add to your collection of wise sayings the sayings we use at times of illness and suffering, such as "Starve a cold, feed a fever."

5

Responding to Pain
Job 29—31; 38—42

Job's entire world has been turned on end. Family, friends, and faith are all torn from the fabric of life. What do we do when our world ends? What does God do?

Personal Preparation
1. Reread the Book of Job.
2. Read and reflect upon Psalm 4:4.
3. With respect to an area of suffering in your life, write a prayer to God that includes the depth and breadth of emotion within your experience.

Understanding
The very structure of the Book of Job asks us to think about how we respond to suffering. At the beginning and ending of the story, the narrator gives us information meant to help sort out the specifics of the story. We learn of Job's innocence and, at the end, his redemption. The rest of the book is filled with human and divine response to pain, anger, and loss.

How are we to find meaning in the innocent suffering of Job? Some interpreters suggest that the ending of the book indicates that the one who suffers will be rewarded through the growth that results from the suffering (42:7-17). Others suggest that the divine speeches from the whirlwind indicate that humans can never fully understand God's ways (38:1—42:6).

Still others emphasize that Job's questioning of God shows us that anger is an appropriate response to suffering and can lead us to a more authentic relationship with God, even within suffering (29—31).

We experience many pains and griefs in life. Suffering is part of the human condition. The deepest pain we can feel, however, is when our world of meaning is collapsing. Our grief is tied to loss—death of family, loss of relationship, job loss, growing up and leaving home. But when we lose our way of making meaning out of the chaos of the world, we experience the deeper crisis. This crisis, what developmental psychologists call dissonance, is invitation not simply to survive the loss, but to be transformed into a new way of being. It makes sense that the Chinese depict the word for crisis by combining the symbols for danger and opportunity.

At about two and a half years, our children underwent a transition of meaning-making. Having developed more complex thought patterns and communication skills, they were no longer satisfied by monosyllabic, noncommittal responses from their parents. For the first time it was no longer possible for us to be in satisfactory dialogue with both children at the same time. Many a "conversation" ended with a child writhing on the ground in inconsolable grief, because she was unfamiliar with the concept of waiting her turn for satisfactory conversation. The tragedy was not that the children were not heard, but that they could no longer count on being heard; their world had changed.

Slowly, but surely, our home has been transformed into a place where each person can be heard in his or her own sacred space. Each one waits their turn (some times more successfully than others). The key to this transition was the phrase "Look at my nose."

Since these new, more complex conversations demanded more deliberate attentiveness, "Look at my nose" meant "pay attention." It was our way of getting our children to focus on something outside themselves. The crisis of not being immediately attended to was resolved by being rewarded for waiting (i.e., a more "grown up" relationship).

Thus, the whole concept of what it means to speak and what it means to listen has changed.

Job is mourning, to be sure, for his family, servants, and property, but he is grieving so deeply because his world of theological meaning has been totally devastated. What begins as a question about fairness broadens into a discussion about God. No longer confined by the cause and effect model, which Job's friends maintain, God is inviting a new theology. This discussion, fueled by pain, forces Job out of his old theology and into a new relationship.

While we can never fully understand God's ways in the world, we are offered some insights about the divine mystery. God's intentional movement toward vulnerability allows this. While we would prefer that God squash evil out of existence, that is not God's way.

At the beginning of Job's story, God turns over control of the situation to the Satan. This action reminds us that God chooses to wrestle with evil and to do so from weakness rather than strength. God's chosen vulnerability is evident in the garden, in exile, and on the cross. It is evident in the Roman Empire, in the concentration camps, and within our churches.

The inherent invitation in a theology that includes a vulnerable God is invitation for relationship. Relationship with an all-powerful being is impossible (at least in the general understanding of relationship). The cries of a suffering person cannot be heard fully by a God incapable of feeling pain. We cannot be called on to risk by a God who is unwilling to risk.

When God chooses to limit divine power, however, we are invited into real relationship. We are invited to change toward God. The story of Job ends with an element that was absent in its beginning—direct communication from God. In his suffering, Job cries for a response from God and he gets it. While Job's "friends" are chastised by God for their invulnerable faiths, it is God's vulnerability that establishes a new relationship with Job.

Unfortunately, invitation into deeper relationship is also invitation into deeper pain. The more loved, the more painful the loss. The more familiar the presence, the more deeply felt the absence. The more invested the couple, the hotter the battle.

Early in my marriage, my mother brought some practical advice. "Couples," she said, "should not be allowed to get married unless they first learn how to fight." Sage advice, from one's mother. If the couple cares about each other, disagreement is inevitable; anger is bound to come.

The story of Job ends, as did the story of Jonah, with one man's anger at God bringing conversation and relationship. While we may not be totally satisfied with God's reaction to Job's lament, that's okay. Our total satisfaction is not God's chief aim. Being totally within relationship is what God is after even and especially in the midst of suffering.

Discussion and Action

1. Share the prayers you wrote at the beginning of this lesson. Ask each person to describe his or her feelings about writing these prayers and sharing them with the group.
2. Discuss your interpretation of Psalm 4:4. What does it mean to be angry but not sin?
3. What does the story of Job and his friends tell us about how we might minister to people whose lives have been affected by the diagnosis of terminal illness?
4. The writer describes the crisis in the lives of his young children when they discovered that they couldn't always have what they wanted. Share early memories of disappointment. How did your disappointments help you find a more realistic understanding of life?
5. Discuss the difference between powerlessness and vulnerability. What does it mean to have a God who chooses to fight evil through vulnerability?
6. Keep adding wisdom sayings to your collection, especially those that deal with pain and suffering.

6

Searching for Meaning in Our World
Ecclesiastes 1:1-18

Ecclesiastes reminds us of the painful truth that blessings do not always follow good behavior. But in the moment of our despair, when all seems meaningless, Ecclesiastes shows us that we can be transformed.

Personal Preparation
1. Read Ecclesiastes 1. What are your feelings after having read it? Are there specific examples from your own life that illustrate the writer's feelings and observations? Have you ever found yourself feeling that "vanity of vanities. All is vanity"?
2. Try putting your feelings about the book of Ecclesiastes into poetry or free verse.
3. When you are feeling hopeless, what do you do to regain hope? What can you do to help someone else who is feeling hopeless?

Understanding

Ecclesiastes is both the title of a book of the Bible and a professional title for the author of the book. In Greek, *Ecclesiastes* means "assemblyman." In Hebrew, it is a word *(Qohelet)* that seems to relate to "assembly." The RSV and KJV translate this Ecclesiastes as "Preacher." The NIV and NRSV use "Teacher."

The NEB translates it as "Speaker." The TEB calls the author "Philosopher." And the New Jerusalem Bible uses "Qoheleth" as a proper name. Whatever his profession—teacher, preacher, or speaker—this person brings the honest lament of an educated, middle-aged (or older) man who painfully reflects upon his life-long search for meaning. " 'Meaningless! Meaningless!' says the Teacher. 'Utterly meaningless! Everything is meaningless' " (1:2 NIV).

The term here translated "meaningless" has been a sticking point in this passage. Some interpreters understand the Hebrew term *hebel* to mean that all of life is in vain, empty, futile, and useless. It is a word used by the skeptic or pessimist. But other interpreters argue that the term should be understood to mean things are "impermanent" or breathlike—in constant flux and change, or chasing after the wind. This is a very important distinction, because the translation a person picks affects the way he or she looks at the entire book of Ecclesiastes (see Kathleen A. Farmer's *Proverbs and Ecclesiastes).* Is the world meaningless and empty of truth? Or is the world in constant change, where meaning is found in fleeting glimpses of truth that dances in the wind?

I'm not so certain that the two interpretations are mutually exclusive. The Hebrew language is full of words that signify more than one thing, making definition difficult on one hand and the meaning rich on the other. *Hebel* implies both skepticism and impermanence. Moreover, *hebel* implies that something can be both vain and changing at the same time.

In my own life skepticism and impermanence are usually closely related. It shows up in our delight over the achievements of our children as they grow and the sorrow of seeing time march on as we watch our children lose their innocence. Observing the changing nature of life often leads to a fair amount of distress. It is difficult to be a bowman when the target is constantly changing. Archers, preachers, teachers, and students would rather work toward stationary targets and goals.

Something new is happening to wisdom writing in Ecclesiastes: the direct relationship between behavior and blessing that we saw in the Book of Proverbs is falling apart in

Ecclesiastes. The most basic sermon of the wisdom tradition—behave well and you will be rewarded—is turned on its proverbial ear by the preacher. "I . . . applied my mind to . . . wisdom" (1:13), says the preacher, "my mind has had great experience of . . . knowledge" (1:16). But even with great quantities of knowledge and wisdom, he realizes that wisdom is a "chasing after wind" (1:17). It is as impossible to capture meaning as it is to capture the wind. In fact, the search for meaning may lead to even greater suffering (1:18). It is a truth shared by more than just our melancholy preacher. The word *vanity* and the concept of chasing after the wind show up in other passages (Job 7:7, 16; Pss. 39:4-6; 62:9; 78:33; 144:4; Isa. 41:29).

What surprises us most in this book is not the image of chasing the wind or the lament of one who feels that life is nothing but vanity, but that this kind of lament actually made it into the Bible. How could it be that a person with so much honest skepticism about life was allowed to speak so loudly? Why are his words counted as scripture? We cannot know for sure. We can only know that this skeptic did make it into the Bible, which shows that the Bible is an amazing book. It is unafraid of tough questions. It introduces us to the very ideas that could undermine our faith before we think of them ourselves, and ultimately it inspires us to hope.

In *Modern Man in Search of a Soul,* psychologist Carl Jung said, "About a third of my cases are suffering from no clinically definable neurosis, but from the senselessness and emptiness of their lives. This can be described as the general neurosis of our time." That was in the 1920s. We too find ourselves in a world of meaningless change and feelings of emptiness at the end of the century.

How do we deal with vanity? Does the church encourage us to share our fears, misgivings, and frustrations? Or does it suggest that we hide our feelings and cover up challenges to traditional optimism?

We face these questions at the place in our lives where what we have been taught fails to match what we have experienced. At those moments, we are either stymied by pessimism or we accept an invitation to rethink what we believe.

This opportunity for choice and change in a person has been part of the formula ever since God placed that tree in the middle of the garden. Throughout the scriptures, in a variety of stories, crises bring opportunities to choose and change. This is no less true for the writings called Wisdom.

The opportunity for choice toward transformation often is represented in biblical imagery as a desert experience, an empty environment devoid of life. God brings us into the desert and there speaks to our hearts of repentance so that we might come back to the Lord (Hos. 2:16; Joel 2:12). The Hebrew people escaped from bondage in Egypt directly into wilderness and choice (Deut. 30). John the Baptist, following Old Testament prophetic form, came preaching repentance in the desert (Matt. 3:1). Even Jesus went to the desert to make choices following his baptism (Matt. 4:1). Personal transformation is the work of choice in the desert of uncertainty and impermanence.

The voice of Qoheleth is often filled with pain. It is a voice with which we can resonate. As with Jesus in the garden (Matt. 26:39-44), Jacob at Jabbok (Gen. 32:24-31), Job at the hands of catastrophe (Job 3ff.), Esther at "such as time as this" (Esth. 4:14-17), and Jonah under the unpredictable plant (Jon. 4:4-11), our moments of understanding and new meaning are often filled with pain.

Yet, as we observed in the story of Job, pain is not an end in itself. Pain invites new relationship and wholeness. Here, too, a world of impermanence is a world of relationship rather than just knowledge, an invitation to fellowship rather than formula-living.

Far from being negative, chasing after the wind is a powerful metaphor for new life and vitality. Wind is captured when we breath it in, and as breath, it is life-giving. But it can only be held for a short time and then it must be released. Every breath is replaced by a second wind—new smells, new texture, new temperature and taste. Over and over and over, with every breath we are revitalized.

From this vantage point, Qoheleth challenges us to follow his example as he rethinks God's presence in life. In the face of change, we rethink our preconceived notions about who God is and what it means to be faithful followers of the great Mystery—what it means to breath deeply, taste life, then release our breath to breathe again.

Discussion and Action

1. How do you interpret the meaning of Ecclesiastes? Do you think the author is struggling with a meaningless world or a world that is always changing? Why?
2. Give an example from your own life of when a seemingly troublesome change in your life gave you new opportunity or transformed you.
3. Proverbs says that if we do the right thing, we will be rewarded. Ecclesiastes says that nothing we do guarantees rewards. Therefore, it is not so important what we do; rather, it is important to simply find meaning in the things that happen. Which is more true for you?
4. How does your church respond to people who express their pain, anger, or skepticism? In what ways might they be encouraged to express their doubts instead of being silenced?
5. With which of the following do you identify most closely: Jacob at Jabbok (Gen. 32:24-31)? Job (Job 3)? Esther (Esth. 4:14-17)? Jonah (Jon. 4:4-11)? or Jesus (Matt. 26:39-44)? Why?
6. Working together, list moments of significant change in your church in the last ten years. In what ways have these changes been life-giving (a breath of fresh air)? In what ways might the congregation have better released the old wind to capture the new? What of the life-giving force of the old breath still resides in the body of the church?
7. Add to your ongoing list conventional wisdom sayings that express some of the same futility or inevitability you find in Ecclesiastes, such as "The only sure things in life are death and taxes."

7

Finding Meaning in a World That Is Not Always Fair
Ecclesiastes 8:10-15; 9:7-10; 12:1-7

If all is vanity and virtue has no reward, then we must live for the moment, says Ecclesiastes. This is not a license for recklessness, however. It is a chance to grasp every available moment to serve and live for God.

Personal Preparation

1. Read Ecclesiastes 3 and 8—12. What is Qoheleth's solution to the problem of impermanence and constant flux? In what ways do you agree with his suggestions? In what ways do you disagree?
2. What has meaning in life besides fairness? Make a list.
3. This week examine the way you live. Do you live mostly by reason and logic, or by impulse and feeling? Jot down some examples of the types of decisions you make this week.

Understanding

Now that we have talked about the impermanence of the world, the vanity of action, and the uselessness of our striving after the wind, what are we to do? How are we to live in a world that is not always as we would wish it to be? Should we follow popular wisdom ("Don't worry, be happy")? Should we try to make the most of life? And just what does it mean to make the most of life?

Qoheleth understood that the proverbial wisdom he had learned could make him "good" like any child who follows instructions, but it could not make him whole. Life is meant to be lived in relationship with God, not simply in robotic obedience to formulas and mechanical observance of religious piety. There is something within creation—the wind of impermanence—that demands that we pay attention and react within the moments of life as they come, one by one.

Qoheleth tells us of his struggle to find meaning in our world of obvious injustice. He invites us along as he searches for truth in the impermanence he finds. He discovers that knowledge and obedience are not enough for fulfillment. In the end, his study of life leads him to preach that we should "eat, drink, and find happiness." In the face of impermanence, death, and meaninglessness, we are to seize the day in its fullness and live with passion (e.g., 2:24-26; 5:18-20; 7:14; 12:1).

In his book *When All You've Ever Wanted Isn't Enough,* Harold Kushner explains Qoheleth's refrain this way:

> If logic tells us that life is a meaningless accident . . . don't give up on life. Give up on logic. If logic tells you that in the long run, nothing makes a difference because we all die and disappear, then don't live in the long run. Learn to savor the moment.

This is the *carpe diem* of Jewish literature. Seize the day! It is not license to "do whatever you want," but a command to "enjoy the moment given by God."

We cannot sneak away from God to seize the day. The twist here is that God is part of the enjoyment of the moment. Qoheleth says, "There is nothing better for mortals than to eat and drink, and find enjoyment in their toil. This also, I saw, is from the hand of God; for apart from him who can eat or who can have enjoyment?" (2:24-25). We are not commanded to live for the moment, but to live for God in the moment. The moments of life are fulfilled not just in joy alone, but by including God in the moment to complete that joy. So too in moments of sorrow or pain. Each moment is an opportunity to live more fully in that season with God.

In January and February several years ago, I came to a point of frustration in my ministry. It seemed that nothing was happening. My congregation and I seemed to be in a lull. We were not producing any new programs, the creative spark had vanished from sermon preparation, and each month's board agenda looked as though it had been copied from the previous month. After years of growth, excitement, and activity, the white-water river had become a stagnant pond.

So, in the dead of winter, with this concern at the top of my agenda, I went to meet with a mentor, a brother in the Benedictine Abbey on the Illinois River. After a day of retreat, worship, and meditation, I impatiently sat with him during the silent evening meal. After the meal was over, we began to discuss the "problem." I unloaded my full agenda of emptiness while Father Gabriel listened to my plight as he peeled an orange left over from dinner.

I described the situation. I shared about my frustration with myself and with the inactivity of the church. I questioned my vocation, my location, and God's intention. My ministry seemed to be a "chasing after the wind" and a feeling of vanity.

After I had shared my emptiness, Gabriel gave me half of his orange and said, "It is a cold winter." He went on to say that the feelings I was having seemed to him to be feelings of winter. We need winter, he explained, in order to prepare ourselves for the new growth of the spring. What looks like death in the winter may actually be preparation for the flower of spring, growth of summer, and harvest of fall.

In my planning, my preoccupation with growth, and my emphasis on activity, I had failed to see that everything has its season (3:1-13). I was failing to live for God in the moment, to seize the day of rest. Without the rest, which my body, my mind, and my God were demanding, I would not be ready for the burdens of a bountiful season of production. Furthermore, I had been missing the chance to celebrate winter. Like people who live in very cold climates, we must do more than tolerate the climate and abide the moments of inactivity. We must eat, drink, and find happiness within them.

Some of this patience comes with age. There is a natural buildup of wisdom as one survives the rhythms of life. For example, now I can make sense of the spring time process of cleaning out the martin house when I was a boy. While I was inclined to put the clean house atop the pole right away, my father made us wait. We needed to wait for the purple martins. If we put the house up too soon, it would quickly fill with sparrows. The time had to be right for the potential of the house to be filled with purple martins.

Too often we find ourselves living for the future or living in the past instead of living in the present. Living only for the future, we grasp for our own elusive dreams. Living in the past, we are often motivated by guilt, fear, and pain. But living in the present requires that we listen for what God is saying and doing in the "now" and celebrate the seasons of life as we live them.

Often we are driven by personal agendas in our desire for action. We tend to place our own timetables ahead of the activity of the Divine. We find ourselves greedily wanting things to come to fruition before their time. And we end up cursing the fig trees for not producing figs out of season (Mark 11:12-14). Qoheleth's wisdom urges us to pay closer attention to the rhythms of life and attend to God's sovereignty within these seasons. "For everything there is a season and a time for every matter under heaven" (Eccl. 3:1).

Discussion and Action

1. What "season" are you going through in your life? What does it mean to "live in the moment" of this season? In what ways could you "seize the day" that the Lord has made?
2. What season is your church going through right now? Name some opportunities the church or your covenant group could seize right now. What keeps you from seizing the day?

3. Discuss the difference between living for the moment and living for God in the moment.
4. List the things you spend more than five hours doing each week. Ask yourself what value each activity has in your life. Put a yes beside the activity if you feel it's justified and a no beside it if you think it's not really justified. How could you adjust your weekly schedule to allow more time to enjoy the gifts it pleases God to give you?
5. How do you know when the rules you live by are absolutely essential or when they are vain laws that will get you nowhere? Name some of each.
6. Close by singing together "Turn, Turn, Turn" or "I Know Not Why God's Wondrous Grace."

8

Wise Advice for the Well-to-Do
Sirach 4:1-10

In wisdom writings we have seen little mention of God. Sirach, however, believed that a life lived wisely was a life offered up in reverence to God. He would say that respect for God cannot be separated from living as God would have us live. An act as simple as giving to the poor is an act of worship.

Personal Preparation

1. Read Sirach 4:1-10. You might say poverty is a condition of having no money and to be poor is a condition of the mind. Which people in your community fit these categories?
2. Picture the poor of your community. What do you know about them personally? What are they like? How, where, and when do you relate to them?
3. As a Christian, what responsibility do you have to the poor?

Sirach 4:1-10

My child, do not cheat the poor of their living,
    and do not keep needy eyes waiting.
²Do not grieve the hungry,
    or anger one in need.
³Do not add to the troubles of the desperate,
    or delay giving to the needy.

⁴Do not reject a suppliant in distress,
  or turn your face away from the poor.
⁵Do not avert your eye from the needy,
  and give no one reason to curse you;
⁶for if in bitterness of soul some should curse you,
  their Creator will hear their prayer.
⁷Endear yourself to the congregation;
  bow your head low to the great.
⁸Give a hearing to the poor,
  and return their greeting politely.
⁹Rescue the oppressed from the oppressor;
  and do not be hesitant in giving a verdict.
¹⁰Be a father to orphans,
  and be like a husband to their mother;
you will then be like a son of the Most High,
  and he will love you more than does your mother.

Understanding

Some people will not find Sirach in their Bibles. It is one of fifteen books that make up the Apocrypha, a collection of scriptures that did not make it into the Bible as we know it. These books were sometimes considered too complicated for most readers or too mysterious (sometimes even heretical) to be included. Today, some versions of the Bible leave the Apocrypha out altogether. Others include it, but put it in a section by itself after the Old Testament.

Sirach, a shortened form of the author's name, is a book of wisdom in the Apocrypha. Sirach recorded his wisdom sayings before 180 B.C. Then after 132 B.C., the thirty-five-verse introduction was written by his grandson who could find no adequate writings in Greek to school young people in wisdom. He translated the entire book into Greek. The book is also known by the titles "Ben Sira" and "Ecclesiasticus" (the more recent Latin title).

While Roman Catholic and Orthodox churches claim this book as scripture, it is not part of the Jewish or Protestant canon. "Hidden" in the Protestant Apocrypha, the book of Sirach does not get much reading time in our churches. This is unfortunate because Sirach is one example of how Judaism shifted immediately prior to the arrival of Jesus the Christ.

In our study of this book, we will focus on the section that records the duties of the believer toward the poor and oppressed. Social justice issues are a central concern of the Bible. These concerns, especially the care for widows, orphans, aliens, and the poor, are seen as standards of measure to which kings, societies, and individuals were held (e.g., Exod. 22:22; Lev. 19:9-10; Job 29:11-16; Prov. 29:14; Isa. 1:17; Matt. 5:3-7; 25:34-46; Jas. 1:27).

With a tone of voice like the prophets and a priestly concern for issues of spirituality, Sirach states wisdom's concern for social justice and religious piety. In a single passage (4:1-10), Sirach provides a helpful corrective to the wisdom tradition that previously mentioned our duty to the poor only in scattered verses, which are easily overlooked. By gathering the sayings about duty to the poor in one passage, Sirach has given them greater importance. Moreover, he has surrounded the concern for the oppressed with an emphasis on spirituality (3:30) and on a personal relationship with God (4:10). These verses directly challenge the reader to do something about the marginalized of society as part of the journey of faith.

This section on duties toward the poor and the oppressed completes the first section of the book of Sirach—a section devoted to the actions of ethics and a program of piety. It includes recognition of God's gift of wisdom (1:1-10), instructions on worship (1:11-30, "fear of the Lord"), duties toward God (2:1-18), duties toward parents (3:1-16), the need for humility (3:17-24), the giving of alms (3:30-31), and duties toward the poor (4:1-10). In this way, Sirach links faith with justice and wisdom with compassion.

I distinctly remember a Sunday not long ago when, after the service had concluded, one of the ushers came up to me and said, "There's a couple here to see you." After exchanging greetings with the parishioners, I made my way to the young couple still sitting alone in the back pew. I recognized them as a couple who had been to see me a year before, asking for financial aid. "Wonderful," I thought. "I don't need this now."

Sunday morning, my congregation has learned, is not a good time to ask me for anything. On the tail of leading worship and delivering a sermon, I tend to balk at any further demands on my time or emotional energy. But these people had the audacity to come to my worship service and ask for money. Here they sat, the indigent of society, asking for more. Don't these people know better than to show up on a Sunday morning? I thought to myself. Don't they know that Sunday is for worship?

One of the deacons, busy counting the morning's receipts in the secretary's office, kept an eye and ear on the situation as I ushered the very pregnant couple into the office and asked them about their situation. The couple needed ten dollars to fill a prescription for the woman's rash. They showed me the prescription. They even showed me the rash. Feeling a bit put out, I pulled ten dollars from my wallet and handed it over.

The couple shook my hand and thanked me. They headed for the door and an usher helped them on their way. The money-counting deacon asked, "Should I take them to the pharmacy?" I said no. There was an uneasiness in both our voices.

Reflecting on the incident, especially in light of Sirach's observation of our duties to the poor, I have to confess my sin. The deacon would certainly have been in full worship of the Divine as he drove that young couple to the pharmacy. Even more so, the congregation would have served the Almighty in a new way had their pastor not delivered a sermon, but instead delivered to them this young couple. Spirituality and justice are not separate issues. Worship and work are connected.

An old story tells of a visitor to a Quaker meetinghouse. He sat next to one of the older men in the gathering. The silence became uncomfortable for the visitor who soon leaned over to his neighbor and asked, "When does the service begin?" To which the older gentleman answered, "As soon as the worship ends."

Sirach was like that uncomfortable visitor. Service, for him, was not an issue separate from our worship. Rather than begrudgingly helping those in dire straits, believers should seize upon the moment as an opportunity to care for a fellow child of God. Do not cheat, keep waiting, grieve, reject, trouble, turn away, or be bitter toward those who are poor or oppressed, says Sirach. And more than this, go out of your way to hear, greet, rescue, and love them as would their father, mother, and their God. Because in so doing, we experience the love of God (4:10).

If this theme sounds familiar, it is because Jesus himself calls us to this kind of care for the poor, but in an even more radical way (Matt. 19:16ff). Jesus links the relationship believers have with the poor to that which they have with God. "Truly, I tell you, just as you did it to one of the least of these who are members of my family, you did it to me" (Matt. 25:40).

Discussion and Action

1. Talk about reading the Book of Sirach. Does it seem different in any way from the official scriptures of the Bible? Why or why not? What authority does it hold for you?
2. As North Americans, the poorest of us have much more material wealth than many millions in other parts of the world. Does this fact require anything of us as Christians? What?
3. What seems worshipful to you about helping others? Name some opportunities for local service where the group could experience both worship and helping others.
4. Think about worship in your congregation or covenant group. How does it promote care for the poor and oppressed? Brainstorm about ways this could be added to your worship.
5. Write to the denomination's office for volunteer ministries and ask for a list of service opportunities. Decide as a group what you will do with that list.
6. Watch a video drama or documentary on homelessness and discuss it.
7. Add wisdom sayings about poetry and wealth to your list. Do they encourage people to help the poor?

9

Friendship
Sirach 6:5-17

Friendships are like our relationship with God in some ways. Both require loyalty, trust, and respect. And if people of faith truly respect God, they will form strong friendships with others of faith. We cannot respect God if we do not respect the body of Christ in the world.

Personal Preparation
1. Read Sirach 6:5-17. What are your own criteria for friendship? In what way are you a friend to God?
2. Spend some time thinking about your friends. What events in your friendships have worked to strengthen the relationships? Do you remember rough times in these relationships?
3. Sirach suggests building up friendship slowly. Do you think good friendship takes time? Why? Which of your friendships came about quickly and which were slower?

Sirach 6:5-17

Pleasant speech multiplies friends,
>and a gracious tongue multiplies courtesies.

⁶Let those who are friendly with you be many,
>but let your advisers be one in a thousand.

⁷When you gain friends, gain them through testing,
>and do not trust them hastily.

⁸For there are friends who are such when it suits them,
    but they will not stand by you in time of trouble.
⁹And there are friends who change into enemies,
    and tell of the quarrel to your disgrace.
¹⁰And there are friends who sit at your table,
    but they will not stand by you in time of trouble.
¹¹When you are prosperous, they become your second self,
    and lord it over your servants;
¹²but if you are brought low, they turn against you,
    and hide themselves from you.
¹³Keep away from your enemies,
    and be on guard with your friends.
¹⁴Faithful friends are a sturdy shelter:
    whoever finds one has found a treasure.
¹⁵Faithful friends are beyond price;
    no amount can balance their worth.
¹⁶Faithful friends are life-saving medicine;
    and those who fear the Lord will find them.
¹⁷Those who fear the Lord direct their friendship aright,
    for as they are, so are their neighbors also.

Understanding

We are in such a hurry. The rewards of life come much too slowly for our taste. So we have fax machines to replace overnight delivery, which, in turn, has replaced express mail. To hurry things along, one phone company claims to connect our long distance calls two seconds faster than any other. And as if those things aren't enough, we feel we must be able to heat up instant coffee in the microwave during a fifteen-second commercial.

    Yet we sometimes learn that the quick and easy path is unfulfilling. In fact, the rapid route is routinely the least rewarding. Simple observation of reality sheds light on this truth in many areas of life, one of which, Sirach points out, is friendship.

    Certainly, "pleasant speech multiplies friends and a gracious tongue multiplies courtesies" (6:5), but delving deeper yields greater rewards. While it is good to surround oneself with

Friendship

friendly people (6:6), not every friendly person is indeed a friend. The friend sought by Sirach is one in a thousand (6:6). And although the friend may be found in good times, the relationship is not firmly established until life goes bad.

We often joke about friendship with each other when losing arguments or discovering differences of opinion. "Well you can sure tell who your friends are," we say with a sarcastic grin. But at the heart of it, the statement has great wisdom. It is not until "times of trouble" that we discover the depth of relationships (6:8, 10). It is not until a crisis that we discover who is willing to build bridges, come to the rescue, or hang in with us rather than abandon us (6:8, 10, 12), gossip about us (6:9), and argue with us (6:12).

Wisdom says that people are fickle. Most who claim to be friends will fall away in the face of trouble. Many will even turn against you when opportunity arises. "Choose carefully," says Sirach. "Gain [friends] through testing, and do not trust them hastily" (6:7). Some things just take time. Some things, like deepening relationships, take tough times.

True friends make a point to arrive when everyone else is leaving. They provide shelter and do not turn with the wind. In a world that threatens loneliness with its momentary gathering of so many human islands within the stormy sea, friends are life-savers (6:16). We soon learn that it is indeed not good for one to be alone (Gen. 2:18).

For Sirach, however, friendship goes even deeper. Friendship is connected to faith. Something about how we relate to God gets translated into how we form friendships (6:16). Something about reverence for God directs our relationships for the better (6:17). It may be too trite to say that we are to be God's friends, but we do recognize that people who have learned to be in relationship with God have the tools needed to be true friends. The loyalty, trust, and respect that make for a good relationship with God are the same elements that make for a good relationship with friends.

In verse 17 Sirach says, "Those who fear the Lord direct their friendships aright." People of faith are people of friendship. Relationships with people are an essential part of our relationship with God. We read about this in 1 John 4:20-21: "Those who say, 'I love God,' and hate their brothers or sisters, are liars; . . . The commandment we have from him is this: those who love God must love their brothers and sisters also."

In some churches Communion and the reenactment of the Lord's Supper are based on this assumption that faith and friendship are connected, that we love the Lord and love our neighbors as ourselves. It used to be that prior to the Lord's Supper the deacons of the church would visit each member, asking if they were in harmony with the rest of the congregation. People who were not in harmony with their brothers and sisters in Christ could not receive Communion. While we tend to view this as a new legalism, they saw it as a way to avoid a contradiction of terms. One could not be unified with God while being divided from the body of Christ. One could not be at peace with God and at war with the fellowship of believers.

We would do well to take this observation seriously in our modern understanding of faith. Reconciliation with our brothers and sisters is not something we do just to feel better. Reconciliation is essential to faith. When angry with each other, when divided by issues or interpretations, when we leave the table of a friend, we leave the table of the Lord (Sirach 6:10).

Friendships of integrity are relationships in which language, luggage, and life experiences are filtered with unconditional love. They are relationships of safety and shelter from storm. They are essential for faith. They are sandwiched between a rich history of life together and a confidence about a steadfast future. They take time and are worth every minute invested.

> O, the comfort—the inexpressible comfort of feeling safe with a person,
> Having neither to weigh thoughts,
> Nor measure words—but pouring them right out—just as they are—
> Chaff and grain together,
> Certain that a faithful hand will take and sift them—
> Keep what is worth keeping—
> And with the breath of kindness blow the rest away.
> —"Friendship" by Dinah Craik

Friendship

Discussion and Action

1. Talk together about friendship. What is a friend? What do we expect of friends? What does it mean to be a friend to others?
2. Tell about a special friendship from your childhood and from adulthood. How are these relationships different from others?
3. Discuss the importance of reconciliation between friends. What should we do when a relationship with a friend breaks down?
4. How does brokenness between church members affect the spiritual life of the congregation? What can the church do to reconcile members so that people can truly honor God? Give examples of reconciliation from your congregation.
5. When have you found reconciliation during the Lord's Supper or Communion?
6. Talk together about the role of the deacons in the church. Should we institute the annual visit of deacons to members in our congregations? Why or why not?
7. Add wisdom sayings about friendship to your growing collection. Which, if any, give the same advice as Sirach?

10

Wise Advice in an Age of Anxiety
Matthew 6:19-34

The New Testament also contains many wisdom sayings, particularly in Matthew and James. To be wise, according to Matthew, is to follow Jesus instead of the world. A life of discipleship is not without its pain, but its reward is freedom.

Personal Preparation

1. Read the Sermon on the Mount (Matthew 5—7). Pay special attention to 6:19-34. On a slip of paper, jot down the points of stress in your life.
2. Indicate on your list the three largest stress points in your life. Pray for insight about these.
3. Who are the "masters" in your life that compete with God for your obedience?

Understanding

Echoes of the wisdom tradition can be heard in the New Testament, especially in Jesus' teachings in the Sermon on the Mount and in the ethical instruction of the Letter of James. The section of the Sermon that we focus on here emphasizes anxiety. Jesus' teaching reflects the wisdom tradition in its concern to give practical advice for everyday living and in its willingness to draw upon personal observations of the natural world as a basis for the wisdom that is offered here.

As a young professional I went to my doctor with the symptoms of a seasoned professional. For several months, I had been experiencing chest pains, heartburn, headaches, dizziness, sleepless nights, shortness of breath, fatigue, and chronic diarrhea. He scheduled some tests and we met to discuss what might be causing these frightening symptoms. Looking up from the test results, he asked, "How committed are you to staying in the ministry?" My problem was stress, but this experience changed my life as fundamentally as a heart attack would have.

Stress and anxiety affect our lives deeply. According to the American Academy of Family Physicians, two-thirds of office visits to family doctors are prompted by stress-related symptoms. Anxiety affects our physical, emotional, and spiritual beings with alarming regularity.

Of course, some stress can be good. The pressure to complete this writing project has served to motivate me and has encouraged some long hours in front of the computer screen. If I did not feel some pressure to complete this assignment, the project would linger on and on. Some stress motivates, encourages, and strengthens our resolve. As the theologian Sören Kierkegaard said, "With the help of the thorn in my foot, I spring higher than anyone with sound feet."

More frequently, however, stress and anxiety tend to get out of hand. They become crippling and cause us to respond in inappropriate ways. Sometimes our bodies slowly destroy themselves when subjected to unrelenting stress. Often our emotional and spiritual lives tend to spiral into darkness when stress and anxiety are out of control. Even without our knowing it, anxiety gnaws away at the very substance of our being.

Sadly, the habits we adopt to help us cope with stress are often as bad for us (or worse) than the stress they set out to alleviate. In college I purchased a motorcycle, which was supposed to be freeing and thrilling. Soon after I bought my bike, I developed a toothache that was putting a crimp in my style, but when I went to the dentist, he could find nothing wrong with my teeth. After we talked about my daily routine to see if anything I was doing could cause my teeth to hurt, we discovered that when riding the motorcycle I was unknowingly clenching my teeth. The resulting strain on my jaw and teeth caused the pain. The thrill of riding a motorcycle, which was supposed to give me so much freedom, was actually bringing more stress to my body.

Many things in our lives are like that motorcycle. Our pursuit for earthly happiness often leads to spiritual deprivation. In Matthew 6, Jesus emphasizes how consumerism and materialism lead to our abandonment of the reign of God. Wealth becomes an end in itself, a god for our worship, a seductive and demonic goal. Materialism is a jealous god—demanding all our attention and causing us to worry about things other than those which bring eternal happiness and life.

It is not that we or our institutions, such as colleges and churches, have consciously chosen to focus on the bottom line or sheer numbers of people, but once we begin to emphasize quantity over quality, we are seduced into placing money and size above everything else. The quest for wealth (financial or numerical) brings darkness and anxiety. It prohibits our ability to live in the reign of God.

The example Jesus gives in 6:24 about the danger of serving two masters is more than a discussion about wealth and worth, finances and faith. Nor is the section that follows a text about getting rid of pain—about how God can help us lead a more relaxed life while pursuing our personal goals. This is not a "don't worry, be happy" methodology; it is the call to faithfulness in a world clamoring for our attention and investment. This is not the "Tums" of faith—a pill to make us feel better when our lifestyle brings discomfort—but a life-orientation that will make us be better.

Jesus teaches that a faithful life is the best stress reducer. In these wisdom sayings in Matthew, Jesus tells again the importance of placing our faith in God first and thus removing worry from life. What we find in these passages is the consistent reminder that devotion to God must be primary and total. We are reminded to seek first the kingdom of God. The fear of God is the beginning of wisdom (Prov. 1:7). In the saying "Today's trouble is enough for today," we see the philosophy of Qoheleth showing through.

Even a life of faith is not without its stresses. But then Jesus did not come to the world to get rid of stress (see Matt. 10:34 and Luke 2:35). Jesus' words, like his life, call us toward a more radical challenge to reorient our lives toward God and to apply our concern where it really counts. It just so happens that, in so doing, those things that once claimed our anxious attention fade from their previous importance.

Kingdom people learn to worry about clothing the naked; they tend not to worry about wearing the latest fashions. Kingdom people learn to listen to the voices of those who are hungry; this makes it hard to spend the day dreaming of culinary delights for themselves. Kingdom people are busy granting God the authority in their lives; they tend to relax their authoritative posture with others. Kingdom people recognize the call to live life; they give up the tension of struggling to survive. Giving God the throne of the heart removes the tyrant-king of shortsighted self-interest, peer pressure, and materialism.

Anyone who observes our feathered friends for very long realizes that Jesus' comment about birds is not entirely accurate. One conversation with the owner of a cherry tree will give proof that birds are tremendous international harvesters. One look at a newly washed car under a flock of roosting sparrows likewise gives tribute to the fair amount of planting done by these winged wonders.

The point is that birds don't spend a whole lot of time worrying about these activities. Nor does it seem to be of great concern that they get their harvest and planting in the wrong order. It is in their natural pursuit of what God created them to be that their harvest and planting benefit the world. Likewise, when people search for and pursue that which God has created them to be, the worries of life fall back into line and the benefit to the world springs forth.

We often confuse doing and being. While we are often tremendously concerned about what we are to be doing, it is who we are and how we are that God cares about. When we discover what it is God would have us be, our doing comes naturally.

Discussion and Action

1. Share your lists of personal stresses. Work with each other to decide which are good stresses and which are bad. Talk about ways you could change.
2. The Sermon on the Mount is a wisdom writing. Which of its verses have been most important in your life? most practical? Consider acting out the Sermon on the Mount or having several readers present it as a sermon to your covenant group.
3. "You have heard that is was said, . . . *but* . . ." As we understand more about Jesus and the gospel, the old wisdom changes. How has your wisdom changed as you have learned to know more about Jesus?
4. Recall your baptism. Renew the covenant you made to be a follower of God's will by repeating baptismal vows found in your denominational worship book or repeating the Christian vows on page 66. Commit together to seek first the reign of God. Reflect on what that might mean for your life and what anxieties could be eliminated from your life.
5. Share times when you have truly placed God first in your life. What difference did it make in your spiritual health?
6. Place a candle in a large metal bowl. Light the candle and allow it to represent Christ's presence within the group. On small slips of paper, write a word or two to signify an anxiety-producing stress that you now carry. Burn the paper in the flame of the candle, and allow the fire to consume the anxiety as the burning paper drops into the bowl.
7. Sing together "Move in Our Midst." Celebrate God's gift of wisdom to "strike the fetters that bind our feet" and "lead us aright."
8. Look over your collection of wisdom sayings. Add any you know about anxiety and stress. Consider appointing someone to type the collection and make copies for the youth in your congregation.

Suggestions for Sharing and Prayer

This material is designed for covenant groups that spend one hour in sharing and praying together, in addition to the hour of Bible study. These suggestions will help relate the group's sharing to their study of *Wisdom*. Session-by-session ideas are given first, followed by general resources.

This guide was compiled by Linda Logan of Bridgewater, Virginia. Linda is a minister of Christian education at the Bridgewater Church of the Brethren.

1. What Is Wisdom?

- ❏ Spend a few minutes greeting each other. Welcome new people in the group; catch up briefly with those who are returning.
- ❏ In this chapter, Christopher Bowman writes about his "call" to the ministry and several factors in his call: the advice of a friend, his enjoyment of things religious, and a natural interest in the Bible. What factors were part of your call to joining this group?
- ❏ By wisdom and powers of observation, we see God revealed in the rhyme and reason of the natural order. Sing or read together "All Things Bright and Beautiful" on page 64. Pray between verses, naming the evidence you see of God in the world, such as mountains, family, or seasons.
- ❏ Have one person pray each of the following sentences, pausing for silent prayer between each one:

  We thank God for the many ways we receive help in our choices.
  We thank God for the advice of good friends.
  We thank God for experience and observation.
  We thank God for deep feelings and strong inclinations.

We thank God for the written word and the example of Jesus.

We thank God for the Spirit's movement in our decision-making.

❑ Or write a prayer litany using the phrases above (or similar ones), following each with "We give you thanks, O God" or "Hear our prayer of thanks, O God."

2. Practical Wisdom

❑ Jot down ten choices you made today (when to get up, what to wear, whether to eat a snack, what to say to someone, etc.). After lists are complete, mark your list as follows:

H—any choice that was governed by habit

N—any choice that was new

I—the most important choice on the list

G—any good choices you made

B—any bad choices you made

?—any choices where time will tell

Some choices may have more than one letter. Discuss your choices with the group. Also, talk about what part wisdom plays in your everyday life?

❑ Tell about a choice that made a difference in your life.

❑ If you are able, talk about any difficult choices you are facing now.

❑ Wisdom scriptures call on people to care for the poor. Name personal choices you could make to relieve someone else of poverty. Talk about why these are hard steps to take sometimes. Encourage each other to take the first step, whatever it might be.

❑ Pray together about people by name who are facing difficult choices.

❑ Sing or read together "Once to Every Man and Nation" (p. 68) or "Savior of My Soul" (p. 63).

Suggestions for Sharing and Prayer 59

3. Wisdom Has Its Rewards

- ❏ For our wise choices, Proverbs says we are rewarded with good health, wealth, safety, faith, contentment, and honor. Tell how you have experienced these rewards in your life.
- ❏ It is suggested that God gives rewards . . .
  a. directly and justly (God as the divine "vending machine")
  b. by creating a universe that automatically rewards good choices
  c. by rewarding faith and trust more than good behavior
  d. by being present to see us through hard times, but not necessarily to spare us

  Which do you think are most true? Give an example from your own experience.
- ❏ In prayer name the ways that God "rewards" or blesses group members. Also, name the ways each person present blesses the group.
- ❏ Sing or read "When We Walk with the Lord" (see p. 13 at the beginning of the lesson; also known as "Trust and Obey"), "Amazing Grace," or "Great Is Thy Faithfulness."

4. When the Innocent Suffer

- ❏ Sing verse two of "When We Walk with the Lord." Are these words harder to sing this week than last? Does the fact of innocent suffering change the meaning of the hymn for you?

    Not a burden we bear, not a sorrow we share,
    but our toil he doth richly repay.
    Not a grief nor a loss, not a frown nor a cross,
    but is bless'd if we trust and obey.
    —John H. Sammis

    Talk about when you or someone else suffered innocently.
- ❏ In your examples of suffering, were there ways "God made the pain something less than the final word in the story"? What were they?

- ❏ "Pain is a part of the human condition within creation." From a box of crayons or markers, choose a color that signifies pain for you. With that color, draw what you think pain looks like.
- ❏ With sentence prayers, ask God your questions about suffering. Struggle with God about people you feel are suffering unfairly. Pause between each prayer for silent reflection.
- ❏ End by praying Psalm 23 from memory or by reading it together. Then sing "Gentle Shepherd" or "In Your Sickness."

5. Responding to Pain

- ❏ Much of the Book of Job tells of the bad advice from Job's friends. Discuss experiences where friends have tried to support you in difficult or tragic situations. Discuss experiences of trying to support others in such situations.
- ❏ Using Psalm 13 as a model, write a lament psalm (see p. 64). Address God. Tell God about your feelings of being treated unfairly. End by reestablishing trust in God. Let those who wish, share their psalms with the group.
- ❏ When did suffering or pain eventually bring you into a closer relationship with God or deepen your faith?
- ❏ Charles Tindley was born to slaves in 1851 and, despite discrimination and poverty, became a pastor and leader among black Christians. Imagine what it is like to suffer and still be able to sing the words of his hymn "When the Storms of Life Are Raging, Stand by Me." Say the words together (as found on pp. 64-65).

6. Searching for Meaning in Our World

- ❏ When have you dared to voice the reality that life seems empty, meaningless, and futile? What were the circumstances?
- ❏ Adolescence, mid-life, and old age are often presented as times when people struggle with the meaning of life. Share experiences from these periods in your life or the life of a family member.

- ❑ The author of Ecclesiastes says impermanence and change are evidence of futility. When has change thrown your life into chaos and caused you to feel that life is futile, if only temporarily?
- ❑ Pray intercessory prayers for people battling feelings of futility. Then pray thanksgiving prayers for things in your life that are so important to you that they give meaning to your life.

7. Finding Meaning in a World That Is Not Always Fair

- ❑ Sing or read together "Count Your Blessings" on page 70.
- ❑ List blessings you have received today, especially ones you may have taken for granted or almost missed.
- ❑ Write your name on an index card or slip of paper and drop it in a box or a hat. When all group members have done this, pass the box and draw out a card, making sure you do not get your own. On the card write a blessing for the person listed there. Bless them with something like an hour each day to spend with family or an hour for doing nothing or an hour to do something for God. Read the cards aloud and then hand them back to the right person.
- ❑ In prayer, ask God to help you take advantage of every moment. Pray in this way: *Dear God, help us not to miss* [name the blessing] *you give especially for us.* After each prayer, say as a group: *Help us live each moment for you.*
- ❑ Sing "Morning Has Broken."

8. Wise Advice for the Well-to-Do

- ❑ Wisdom literature teaches that caring for the poor is a part of the lifestyle of the wise. Talk about times you have shared with others. When have others shared with you? What did you learn in sharing or receiving?
- ❑ Discuss your reactions to the following quotations:

   "How can I eat cake when my neighbor has no bread?" (Dan West)

"We must live simply in order that others may simply live." (Unknown)

"If I have more than I need and my neighbor has less than he needs, then I am a thief." (Gandhi)

❏ Sing or read "Brothers and Sisters of Mine Are the Hungry" as a prayer (see p. 65).

❏ As a group compose several proverbs expressing what you know or believe about wealth and poverty. A proverb could begin:

If we love God we will . . .
The wise person . . .
Wealth is . . .

Try writing your proverbs on small pieces of plain self-adhering shelf paper cut into shapes. Use these as stickers for correspondence, bumper stickers, notebooks, and lapels.

❏ Pray about your stewardship of the material blessings you control. Then in silence for three to five minutes, listen carefully for God's answers to your prayers.

9. Friendship

❏ On a piece of paper, plot the times you spent with friends this week. What did you discover about the importance of friends in your life?

❏ Think of a good friend of yours. Then discuss some of the following: How did the friendship begin? How long has it lasted? Have you been through difficult times together? What do you contribute to the friendship? What do you receive? Has forgiveness ever been a part of the experience?

❏ How is God like a friend? How is friendship with God different from a human friendship?

❏ Read aloud "I Had a Friend" (see p. 65-66). Then sing "What a Friend We Have in Jesus."

❏ Thank God in prayer for each friend you can count on. Ask God's help in being a friend to those who count on you. Give thanks to God for being your friend.

Suggestions for Sharing and Prayer

10. Wise Advice in an Age of Anxiety

- When has stress spurred you on to something good? When has stress made you withdraw or become ineffective?
- Talk about ways you usually deal with stress. Are any of these methods counterproductive? Which ones? Share your constructive methods with the group.
- Mention the meaningful work you do for God that keeps you from getting bogged down in trivial worries. Or mention the stresses of church work that lead to burnout. Have a time of prayer in which you can pray aloud for members of the group, praying that they will have wisdom to balance the activities in their lives.
- Read Matthew 6:25-34 aloud as a prayer.
- Read the wisdom sayings you have been collecting as a closing litany. Each person can read one and pass the list on around the circle until all have been read. Close by reading or singing "It Is Well," "Cast Thy Burden Upon the Lord," or "O God in Restless Living."

General Sharing and Prayer Resources

Savior of My Soul

Savior of my soul, let me choose thy goal.
Self to thee I would surrender,
choose thy cross, be thy contender.
Let me choose thy goal, Savior of my soul.

Christ, extend thy hand, for I cannot stand.
Thy soul's pow'r, O share with me,
and I thy foll'wer close will be.
I am too weak to stand; Christ, extend thy hand.

Jesus, grant me grace so to run my race,
that I may victorious be.
Thy favor show and prosper me.
So as I run my race, Jesus, grant me grace.
    —John Naas

Psalm 13

[1]How long, O Lord? Will you forget me forever?
    How long will you hide your face from me?
[2]How long must I bear pain in my soul,
    and have sorrow in my heart all day long?
How long shall my enemy be exalted over me?
[3]Consider and answer me, O Lord my God!
    Give light to my eyes, or I will sleep the sleep of death,
[4]and my enemy will say, "I have prevailed";
    and my foes will rejoice because I am shaken.
[5]But I trusted in your steadfast love;
    my heart shall rejoice in your salvation.
[6]I will sing to the Lord,
    because he has dealt bountifully with me.

When the Storms of Life Are Raging

When the storms of life are raging, stand by me;
when the storms of life are raging, stand by me.
When the world is tossing me, like a ship upon the sea,
thou who rulest wind and water, stand by me.

In the midst of tribulation, stand by me;
in the midst of tribulation, stand by me.
When the hosts of hell assail, and my strength begins to fail,
thou who never lost a battle, stand by me.

In the midst of faults and failures, stand by me;
in the midst of faults and failures, stand by me.
When I've done the best I can, and my friends misunderstand,
thou who knowest all about me, stand by me.

In the midst of persecution, stand by me;
in the midst of persecution, stand by me.
When my foes in war array, undertake to stop my way,
thou who saved Paul and Silas, stand by me.

When I'm growing old and feeble, stand by me;
when I'm growing old and feeble, stand by me.

When my life becomes a burden, and I'm nearing chilly Jordan,
o thou Lily of the Valley, stand by me.
—Charles A. Tindley

Brothers and Sisters of Mine Are the Hungry

Brothers and sisters of mine are the hungry,
who sigh in their sorrow and weep in their pain.
Sisters and brothers of mine are the homeless,
who wait without shelter from wind and from rain.

Strangers and neighbors, they claim my attention.
They sleep by my doorstep, they sit by my bed.
Neighbors and strangers, their anguish concerns me,
and I must not feast till the hungry are fed.

People are they, men and women and children,
and each has a heart keeping time with my own.
People are they, persons made in God's image,
so what shall I offer them, bread or a stone?

Lord of all living, we make our confession:
Too long we have wasted the wealth of our lands.
Lord of all loving, renew our compassion,
and open our hearts while we reach out our hands.

By Kenneth I. Morse, copyright 1974, Church of the Brethren
General Board. Used by permission.

I Had a Friend

I had a friend; I don't think that we're friends any more. I'm not sure what happened. I missed a few of our appointed meetings. I felt sure he'd understand. A couple of times when we were talking, I saw some others approach and gave them my full attention, forgetting my friend. I felt sure that he'd understand. I didn't see him for a couple of weeks, but then when I did see him, I was careful to be enthusiastic and pretend we'd seen each other more often. He moved away. I wrote regularly for awhile, but then ... well, you know how it is. I'm sure he knew how busy I was. I felt sure that he knew I thought of him often. I sent him a birthday card. It was a week late, but it was a funny one, and I was sure he would understand. I heard recently that he'd had some bad luck. I really felt very sorry. I'd like to send him a note, just to let him know that I care, for we were really very close, you see. As it happens, however, I can't find his address.

Last night I went to a church service, and during it we sang the old hymn "What a friend we have in Jesus." I felt strangely embarrassed.

From *God Is No Fool* by Lois A. Cheney. Copyright 1969
Abingdon Press. Used by permission.

My Christian Vows

I do believe that Jesus Christ is God's Son and do receive Him and trust Him as my Savior.

I will turn away from all sin and will endeavor by God's grace to live according to the example and teachings of Jesus.

I will be loyal to the church, upholding her by my prayers, my presence, my substance, and my service.

Suggestions for Sharing and Prayer 67

All Things Bright and Beautiful
ROYAL OAK 76.76 with refrain

All things bright and beau-ti-ful, all crea-tures great and small,
all things wise and won-der-ful, the Lord God made them all.

1. Each lit-tle flow'r that o-pens, each lit-tle bird that sings,
God made their glow-ing col-ors, God made their ti-ny wings.

2. The pur-ple-head-ed moun-tain, the riv-er run-ning by,
the sun-set, and the morn-ing that bright-ens up the sky;

3. The cold wind in the win-ter, the pleas-ant sum-mer sun,
the ripe fruits in the gar-den, God made them ev-'ry one.

4. God gave us eyes to see them, and lips that we might tell
how great is God Al-might-y, who has made all things well.

*Guitar chords for unison singing only

Text: Cecil F. Alexander, 1848, alt.
Music: English melody, 17c., adapted by Martin Shaw, 1915
Harmonization copyright © renewed 1983 John Ribble. Used by permission.

Once to Every Man and Nation

EBENEZER (Ton-Y-Botel). 8787D

1. Once to ev'ry man and nation Comes the moment to decide, In the strife of truth with falsehood, For the good or evil side; Some great cause, some great decision Offering each the bloom,

2. By the light of burning martyrs, Christ, Thy bleeding feet we track, Toiling up new Calvaries ever With the cross that turns not back. New occasions teach new duties, Time makes ancient

3. Though the cause of evil prosper, Yet 'tis truth alone is strong. Though her portion be the scaffold, And upon the throne be wrong, Yet that scaffold sways the future, And, behind the

Text: James Russell Lowell, 1819-1891, alt.
Music: Welsh hymn melody

Suggestions for Sharing and Prayer

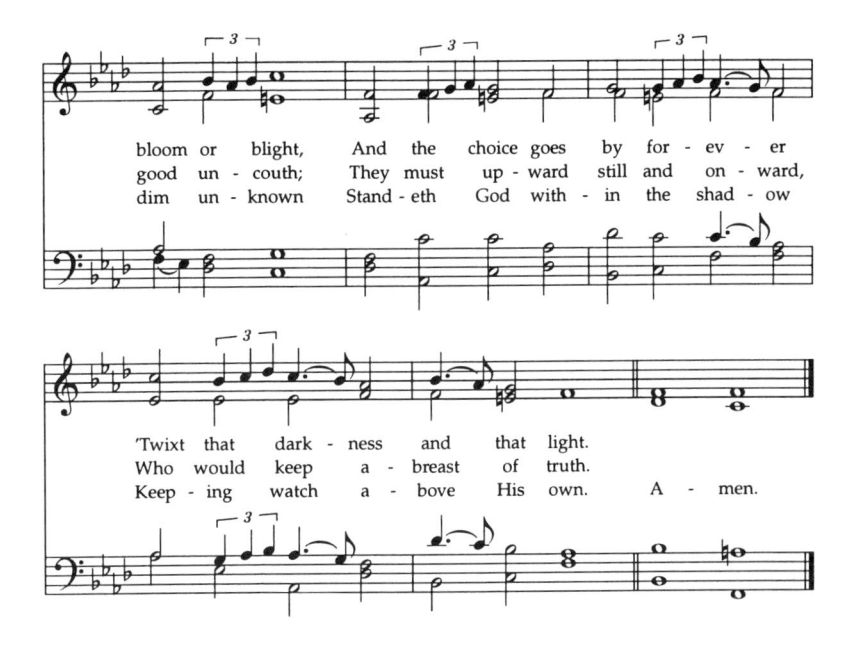

bloom or blight, And the choice goes by for - ev - er
good un - couth; They must up - ward still and on - ward,
dim un - known Stand - eth God with - in the shad - ow

'Twixt that dark - ness and that light.
Who would keep a - breast of truth.
Keep - ing watch a - bove His own. A - men.

Count Your Blessings

1. When upon life's billows you are tempest-tossed,
When you are discouraged, thinking all is lost.
Count your many blessings, name them one by one,
And it will surprise you what the Lord hath done.

2. Are you ever burdened with a load of care?
Does the cross seem heavy you are called to bear?
Count your many blessings, ev'ry doubt will fly,
And you will be singing as the days go by.

3. When you look at others with their lands and gold,
Think that Christ has promised you His wealth untold;
Count your many blessings, money cannot buy
Your reward in heaven, nor your home on high.

4. So amid the conflict, whether great or small,
Do not be discouraged, God is over all;
Count your many blessings, angels will attend,
Help and comfort give you to your journey's end.

Text: Johnson Oatman, Jr., 1856-1926
Music: Edwin O. Excell, 1851-1921

Suggestions for Sharing and Prayer

Other Covenant Bible Studies available from *faithQuest*

Forming Bible Study Groups
Abundant Living: Wellness from a Biblical Perspective
Biblical Imagery for God
Covenant People
Disciplines for Spiritual Growth
Ephesians: Reconciled in Christ
1 Corinthians: The Community Struggles
In the Beginning
James: Faith in Action
Jonah: God's Global Reach
The Life of David
The Lord's Prayer
Love and Justice
Many Cultures, One in Christ
Mystery and Glory in John's Gospel
Psalms
Presence and Power
Real Families: From Patriarchs to Prime Time
Revelation
Sermon on the Mount